COMPLETE
WINDOWS 10
TRICKS BOOK

Easy Way to Master all Windows 10 Shortcuts

Including:

Windows 10 secrets and Aids to remember all Windows 10 tips

PETER MAXWELL

Copyright© 2019

ACKNOWLEDGMENT

I want to say a big thank you to my wife for her invaluable support.

Table of Contents

INTRODUCTION --------------------------------- 9
SECTION ONE ---------------------------------- 12
INTRODUCING THE WINDOWS 10 ------- 12
CHAPTER 1 ------------------------------------ 13
   Windows 10 ----------------------------------- 13
CHAPTER 2 ------------------------------------ 16
   Real great features --------------------------- 16
SECTION 2 ------------------------------------- 23
THE SET UP ----------------------------------- 23
CHAPTER 3 ------------------------------------ 24
Setting up windows 10 ------------------------- 24
CHAPTER 4 ------------------------------------ 27
   Set up windows 10 -------------------------- 27
CHAPTER 5 ------------------------------------ 30
   Basic section --------------------------------- 30
CHAPTER 6 ------------------------------------ 31
   Network section ----------------------------- 31
CHAPTER 7 ------------------------------------ 33
   Account section ----------------------------- 33
CHAPTER 8 ------------------------------------ 39

Privacy options ---------------------------------- 39
SECTION THREE -------------------------------- 43
TIPS AND TRICKS FOR THE WINDOWS 10 --- 43
#TRICK 1 -- 44
How to customize the Start menu --------- 44
#TRICK 2 -- 47
Type with your voice ------------------------- 47
#TRICK 3 -- 48
Get the alternate Start menu --------------- 48
#TRICK 4 -- 50
Use the desktop button ---------------------- 50
#TRICK 5 -- 53
Rotate screen ----------------------------------- 53
#TRICK 6 -- 54
Remove a tile ----------------------------------- 54
#TRICK 7 -- 56
Right-clicking on taskbar -------------------- 56
#TRICK 8 -- 57
Cortana's hidden game ---------------------- 57
#TRICK 9 -- 58
Drag to pin -------------------------------------- 58
#TRICK 10 -------------------------------------- 60

Shake to clear ---------------------------------- 60
TRICK 11 -- 62
Transparent Command Prompt window - 62
#TRICK 12 --- 65
Use focus assist to silence notifications -- 65
#TRICK 13 --- 67
Pin the favorite contacts --------------------- 67
#TRICK 14 --- 69
Close sharing --------------------------------- 69
#TRICK 15 --- 71
Mixed Reality Viewer ------------------------ 71
#TRICK 16 --- 73
File Explorer Dark mode --------------------- 73
#TRICK 17 --- 75
Light mode ------------------------------------ 75
#TRICK 18 --- 77
The new Clipboard --------------------------- 77
#TRICK 19 --- 79
Capture with the screen capture tool ----- 79
#TRICK 20 --- 81
The unknown game bar --------------------- 81
SECTION FOUR -------------------------------- 83
WINDOWS 10 SHORTCUTS ---------------- 83

6

CHAPTER 9 84

   40 Windows 10 Shortcuts 84

   SHORTCUT 1 87

   SHORTCUT 2 91

   SHORTCUT 3 93

   SHORTCUT 4 95

   SHORTCUT 5 97

   SHORTCUT 6 98

   SHORTCUT 7 100

   SHORTCUT 8 103

   SHORTCUT 9 104

   SHORTCUT 10 105

   SHORTCUT 11 106

   SHORTCUT 12 108

   SHORTCUT 13 109

   SHORTCUT 14 110

   SHORTCUT 15 113

   SHORTCUT 16 115

   SHORTCUT 17 116

   SHORTCUT 18 118

   SHORTCUT 19 119

   SHORTCUT 20 122

   SHORTCUT 21 123

SHORTCUT 22 ---------------------------------- 125
SHORTCUT 23 ---------------------------------- 127
SHORTCUT 24 ---------------------------------- 129
SHORTCUT 25 ---------------------------------- 131
SHORTCUT 26 ---------------------------------- 132
SHORTCUT 27 ---------------------------------- 133
SHORTCUT 28 ---------------------------------- 135
SHORTCUT 29 ---------------------------------- 137
SHORTCUT 30 ---------------------------------- 138
SHORTCUT 31 ---------------------------------- 141
SHORTCUT 32 ---------------------------------- 143
SHORTCUT 33 ---------------------------------- 144
SHORTCUT 34 ---------------------------------- 145
SHORTCUT 35 ---------------------------------- 148
SHORTCUT 36 ---------------------------------- 150
SHORTCUT 37 ---------------------------------- 151
SHORTCUT 38 ---------------------------------- 152
SHORTCUT 39 ---------------------------------- 153
SHORTCUT 40 ---------------------------------- 155
DISCLAIMER ---------------------------------- 156
About the Author ---------------------------- 157

INTRODUCTION

Arguably, the most popular computer operating system – Windows OS- continues to make wave in the market. Not only that, new versions of the OS are continuously being rolled out for users to enjoy.

Interestingly, each version comes with added new tricks and tips that users must know to enjoy the experience of the windows OS.

The latest Windows OS presently is the Windows 10. This version came with **numerous shortcuts, overwhelming**

features and mind blowing tricks. But some of these tricks are not readily available to the public. Microsoft decided to leave some as **windows 10 secret**

However the conundrum is: "How can we discover and master these tips so that we can greatly utilize the features of the Windows 10"?

This book is written to provide solution to that problem. Every shortcut and tip written in this book has been subjected to series of trials on every upgrade of the windows 10 different brands of computers.

So sit back, relax and enjoy another wonderful book from the stables of the world renowned tech guru for both beginners and seniors of the Windows 10.
:

SECTION ONE

INTRODUCING THE WINDOWS 10

CHAPTER 1
Windows 10

When we say Windows 10, it's clear what we're talking about. It's an operating system created by Microsoft for computers.

You may also know that it is not the first of their works in this field. In fact, they have created a number of OS versions before Windows 10.

The ones that came earlier include: Windows XP, Windows 7 and Windows 8. Then we have the recent Windows 10. This was released in 2015 and it was widely accepted, just like its predecessors.

When it comes to operating systems, Windows took the early lead, kept the pace and continues to lead down to this day.

So, no one is surprised when Windows 10 gained speed from onset, and retained the momentum.

Often, Windows 10 gets upgrades and users can get the build at no extra cost, that is, for those who want it. We also have the features that are available to Windows

Insiders, like the option to receive other test builds.

CHAPTER 2
Real great features

The support for Universal Apps is one of the greatest features of the Windows 10. These Universal Apps are created to function on tablets, smartphones, X-Box One, PCs, gaming consoles and others.

There are many things that the Windows 10 is capable of doing, when given the right commands to them.

There was a revision in the user interface of Windows and this made it possible for some kind of interactions between touchscreen interface and the mouse-user interface. For the two interfaces, there's a new **Start menu**.

And with the Windows 10 came the **Microsoft Edge**. For many, it serves as a good replacement for the older Internet Explorer. It has got a clean and modern interface that makes browsing easier and it's very different from Explorer.

You can still access Explorer, but when you run the Windows 10, you really don't have any reason to. Microsoft Edge provides you with all you need in a browser. You could say that Edge gives the edge.

When Windows 10 was released in 2015, it got many positive reactions and reviews, all for good reasons. Many applauded the decision of Microsoft to give a **desktop-type** of interface which contrasts with the tablet-type of interface for Windows 8.

Then there was also the integration for **Xbox live**. And let's not forget the lovely **Cortana**. With Windows 10, you can now enjoy the full capability and functionality of the **voice assistant**.

In the **Start**, there are some elements in the Windows 7 that were brought and merged to the Windows 10. Then the titles arrangement of the Windows 8 too was also incorporated. But nonetheless, when you take a look at the **Start interface**, you'll be able to tell that it's been upgraded and not like the older Windows OS.

In the Windows 10, the new Start menu also has other features. The system icons on the operating systems were changed. You can view a list of options and **most used titles** on the left area.

Then on the right of the menu which shows up when you click start, you have a couple of applications. There's also another cool thing about this Start menu; it can be resized. If the menu is too big for your taste, you can just put your cursor near **the top or side of the menu and drag to reduce**.

Then for the tablet mode, the menu will be enlarged to full-screen mode. You also have a new virtual desktop option. Then there's the display for **Task view** that will show you all the tabs that are open and the best part is that you can switch through them. And if you want, you can also switch between different work spaces.

Then the Universal Apps that could only run on full screen display became also available to be used on Windows that are self-contained just like the other apps and programs.

In addition, there's also the option to set program windows into parts of the screen when you drag them to the corner of the display.

Another cool feature is that when you set a window to one part of the screen, you can select another window that will fill up that empty other area.

When the task view appears, you just click the other app that you want to fill the screen and you will have two Windows side by side. This what they call **Snap Assist.**

SECTION 2

THE SET UP

CHAPTER 3

Setting up windows 10

With every revision that the Windows 10 gets, things get changed and moved around. Sometimes, this change could really solve a problem, other times it could prove to be useless or probably create one.

But if you've just got yourself a new computer and you have the Windows 10 **Creators Update** already installed or you want to install it newly by yourself, what you will get with Windows 10 is what they call **Out Of the Box Experience**.

When they say Out Of the Box Experience, they mean the first experience that'll get you to perform certain tasks before you can actually begin to use the computer.

Together with the Out Of Box Experience (OOBE from now on), you will need to connect to a Wi-Fi network, select your language, choose your own account and change the privacy settings.

For the new OOBE, you get more than just the normal change in the display. You are also able to modify and edit your Windows Privacy options better.

If you would like to have control of the information that is shared with developers, the process has become ever so transparent now.

So if you are looking to set up your Windows and see the other changes available, we are going to cover them here.

CHAPTER 4

Set up windows 10

For those that want to perform something like an upgrade from a previous version of Windows; it could be Windows 7 or Windows 8, there won't be the option for OOBE.

But you will get a screen that will tell you about the main and primary apps like Movies & TV, the new Microsoft Edge, Photos and others

On the other hand, if you are setting up a newly bought computer or you are doing a clean install, what you will find is a simple and new interface that will be in 4 sections.

These include, Network, services, Basic and Account. You will also be greeted by **Cortana**; Microsoft's voice assistant. With **Cortana,** you can give out voice commands and you'll be guided through each step.

However, the help that you can get from Cortana is not compulsory. And in fact, if you don't want the assistant, you can just hit the **microphone icon** that is at the bottom-left area.

If you want to adjust the volume, you will also find this option there. The new interface should not be hard to get by and you should have no problem with working through it.

CHAPTER 5
Basic section

From the **Basic** screen, you will be able to select your keyboard and language.

The option to choose another keyboard layout can be really helpful if you are from another region.

CHAPTER 6
Network section

The next screen is for **Network**. And as the name implies, this will have you connecting your device to a network.

If you have an active connection, this option will become available. If you don't, you can just hit **Skip for now**.

If you have a wireless network that you can connect to, just choose it, and hit **Connect**. You will also need to enter your password if it is pass-worded.

But if you are not connected to a wireless network with let's say unlimited data, but a metered connection and don't want to use up much mobile data, you can just select **Properties** and turn on the toggle for **On** just below **Metered Connection**.

CHAPTER 7
Account section

Now we get to the other screen; **Account**. This is important so be sure to fill it out precisely. This is where you get the opportunity to set your **username**. This will be the username that will be used to sign in to your computer and to manage the device.

There are 2 methods that Windows 10 gives you to sign in; **Microsoft account** and **Local account**.

You will only be able to continue set up for your Microsoft account if there is internet connection. But if there is no internet connection available, you will just be prompted to use a Local account.

Using a Local account: If you have earlier versions of Windows like the Windows 7, the Local account works just like it. But you should know that when you use a Local account, you won't be eligible for the perks that someone using a Microsoft account will receive.

For example, the option to download applications from the

Windows Store, PC Sync two-factor authentication will not be available. But when you set up your Local account, you will asked to include a hint, just in case you lose the password.

Using Microsoft account: Now, this is the kind of account that uses a Microsoft email address and this will be connected to your Microsoft account.

The email address could be something like, @live.com or @Hotmail.com, @outlook.com or @msn.com. But you can still set up you Windows with other accounts like @yahoo.com, @iCloud.com or @Gmail.com. You just want to make sure that the email is linked with your Microsoft account.

When you use a Microsoft account, you get the advantage of many settings and file storage. Also your apps will be synced across all the devices that use Windows 10, your passwords as well as themes. Using a Microsoft account also makes you eligible for two-factor authentication and this will protect you from hackers.

The option for **Find My Device** can also be accessed. This service is really useful in case your device gets lost or even worse; stolen. And if you want to be able to download Universal Apps, you will need a Microsoft account. If you want to reinstall Windows 10, a Microsoft account also make reactivation easier.

By now, you may be consider your decision to use a Local account. You have a lot to gain using a Microsoft account. But whatever you choose, you want to ensure that it is safe and secure. Like for example, you don't want to use certain birthdays, names or places of people as your password.

And you don't want to forget your password. Yes, it happens to the most careful of us, but there are still some things you can do to prevent it. You could set aside a secret journal to write your passwords and lock it in a hidden safe. Or you may try to memorize it and know it better than your name.

CHAPTER 8
Privacy options

With the privacy page, you get a list of the option that you can activate. Depending on your preference, some of the options here can take your Windows 10 experience to the next level.

For example, when you use **Location**, you will be able to ask for help from Cortana so that you can get directions.

To help improve some applications on your Windows, Diagnostics can be a good option to try out. Still yet, you may decide to turn off some settings like Relevant Ad and Tailored Experience. You can just hit the **Learn more** option for each of the items on the list if you want to get more info about them. When all is done, select **Accept**

Now your settings will be confirmed by Windows. Windows will then do some processess and last minute Windows updates. It will also check the Windows Store if it can find any latest update.

When you are shown the desktop, you may begin to use Windows 10.

If there was a privacy setting you chose wrongly and want to change the option, you can go back and make adjustment;

    1. By going to **Start**

    2. Choose **Settings**

    3. Select **Privacy**

You can also change some things to suit your taste. For example, if the text is too big or small for you, you can make it bigger or reduce it to your liking. To make some customizations on Windows 10;

    1. Go to **Settings**

2. Choose **System**

3. Then **Display**

4. Select the options to **Change the size of text.**

You can also change the resolution, customize the lock screen, and change the look of the Start menu or even the whole desktop itself. You have the Windows 10 on your PC, the world is your oyster.

SECTION THREE

TIPS AND TRICKS FOR THE WINDOWS 10

#TRICK 1
How to customize the Start menu

The Start menu on your Windows 10 is like the key to any door on your computer. With it, you are able to access applications, settings, and important files. The fact that the menu is just one touch away at the bottom left corner too is just fantastic.

And even if that is too far for you, you have the Windows key on your keyboard. It's the button with the same icon as the Start menu. You can do some customizations in the Start menu to make it seem more cool you.

To do this,

1. Enter the **Settings**

2. Go to **Personalization**

3. Select **Start**. You can choose from the different options that is presented.

    - Show most used apps

    - Show recently added apps

    - Use start full screen

- Then another option to Choose which items shows up on start

#TRICK 2
Type with your voice

You can now type with your voice on Windows 10. Yes, I'm not kidding. You can actually do what they call **Speech Typing**. With the Windows 10, the accuracy to recognize speech was actually increased by Microsoft.

1. Enter the **Settings**

2. Choose **Privacy**

3. Select **Speech**

#TRICK 3

Get the alternate Start menu

You may be interested in using the non-tiled version of the Start menu. Well I wouldn't say straight up that you can get that feature because you can't go into some setting and make the Start change its form. But if you want to get that effect, just right click the Start icon.

This is the Windows icon at the lower left corner of the screen. You'll get the text and listed version for the basic destinations on the Start. This may include Power and

Features, Power Options, Devices Manager, Mobility Center and Command Prompt.

You can get all of these options in the regular tiled version of the Start menu, but if you want to reach them quicker, this is an option.

#TRICK 4

Use the desktop button

If you are familiar with the desktop button, you know that it was really handy in Windows 7. If you don't know this, this is the secret button that you may have stumbled on at one time.

It is at the very corner of the lower right. It's right there, after the date and time. When you click it all your windows are minimized and you'll see the desktop.

But if you just want get a peek of the desktop without permanently minimizing the windows, you can enter the settings and tweak things. You can set it so that you don't have to click the button to view the desktop.

If you just hover on the icon, the desktop will be shown to you. And immediately you remove the cursor from the button, you get all the windows back.

1. Get to the **Settings**

2. Choose **Personalization**

3. Select **Taskbar**

4. Choose **Use peek to preview desktop**

#TRICK 5
Rotate screen

If you would like to have some fun, you can rotate your screen to face all four directions with a quick shortcut. Use **Ctrl + Alt + D + Arrow button**. The arrow button could be any of the four arrows on your keyboard.

If you use the **Down** button, the screen will rotate and face bottom. Use the **Up** arrow to return to normal. Left and right buttons do just the same.

#TRICK 6
Remove a tile

If you are in the Start menu, you'll find some applications that appear as tiles on the screen. These are meant to serve as shortcuts and can be a real shortcut sometimes. But you won't be needing all the apps given by default.

If you want to remove a tile, you can just right click the app and you'll be shown the option to **unpin from start**.

If the app is also pinned to your taskbar, you can also choose **Unpin from taskbar** to remove it.

#TRICK 7

Right-clicking on taskbar

When you do this, you get a menu that gives you the option to reach some features.

This can be **Cortana, Toolbar preset, Task manager or the option to lock taskbar.**

#TRICK 8
Cortana's hidden game

If you look at it in the raw sense, this can't be classified as a real game. They are not as fun as the 3D games you know of.

I think Time-Killers is a more fitting name. Just something to have some fun with Cortana.

You could say or type **Rock Paper Scissors** in Cortana and have a little fun. You could also try something else like **Flip the Coin** or **Roll The Die**.

#TRICK 9
Drag to pin

While this feature was available in Windows 7, Windows 10 got some more upgrades. It's just as simple as taking a window and dragging it to a side of the screen. This will get it to fit half of the screen.

You can also drag that window to any of the corners of the screen. This is helpful if you want your window to fill up quarter of the screen instead of half.

If you make use of multiple screens, you can drag the window to a corner and a prompt will come up to request if the window should show up in that corner.

Another way that you can achieve the same result is pressing **Windows key + Arrow key**. And yes, this can be any of the arrow keys.

#TRICK 10
Shake to clear

This feature was available since Windows 7 and even in Windows 10, it's still available. Yet only a few people know and work with it. But you should use it as it is fun and useful. This is the option to shake a window.

If your desktop is cluttered with different open windows, **you can just take the top of a window you don't want to remove, shake it** and the rest of the windows will be minimized.

If you would like to bring back the windows you minimized, you can just shake back again and it will show up.

TRICK 11

Transparent Command Prompt window

Not many will find this feature useful but for those who would like to dig into the nooks of the hidden Windows closet in the Command Prompt, there's a transparent way that you can go about it.

If you would like to access the Command Prompt, you can use the search in the Start and type in **Command Prompt** and it appear, click it. Another way is to right click the start and select **Command Prompt** option.

1. When you have the Command Prompt window open, right click the top bar

2. Choose the option for **Properties**

3. Now you will see some tabs at the top of the window, choose the **Color** tab

4. Among the number of personalization features that you get, you'll find the slider for **Opacity**. Yours should be set to 100 percent.

You can reduce it all the way to 30 and you'll be able to see through the Command Prompt window

#TRICK 12
Use focus assist to silence notifications

You might know this as **Quiet hours**. But in an update in April 2018, the **Focus Assist** feature allow you to have much more control of the notifications that show up on your computer.

1. Enter the **Settings**

2. Move to **System**

3. Select **Focus Assist**

You can then customize the notifications for apps, contacts and even some particular alarms.

#TRICK 13

Pin the favorite contacts

There's the option to pin your favorite and dearest contacts in the taskbar. This will show up just as when you pin an app to the taskbar.

If you would like to do this,

1. Select the icon for People

2. When you look in the lower part of the popup window, you will find an option to look for contacts and pin them to your taskbar

3. If you don't find any contacts, you can just select the tab for **Apps** at the top and you'll be able to connect to Skype, Mail, or other applications that you will be able to import contacts from.

#TRICK 14
Close sharing

For your photos or documents, you can now share them with other devices as far as the devices are nearby.

If you are familiar with the **AirDrop** with Apple, this shouldn't be new to you.

To make use of it:

1. Select the **Share** icon. You'll find this at the top of the photo toolbar or doc. This will open up the panel

2. Choose turn on **Nearby Sharing** and you will be able to see the recipients that are nearby.

#TRICK 15

Mixed Reality Viewer

In your Windows 10, you have **Mixed Reality Viewer** app that was installed by the Windows Fall Creators Update. Now this is renamed **as 3D Viewer**. If you would like to open it up. You can just search for it in Cortana.

When the app opens, you can just do a quick tour on the 3D models. These could be the ones that are downloaded from the Microsoft library or the one made in Paint 3D.

This app is one way to level up if you would like to play around with some mixed reality production.

#TRICK 16

File Explorer Dark mode

From the Start menu, you get the **Dark mode**. In fact for some time now, it's not only the Start menu that has gotten this customization feature. It's available for some apps, the action center and the taskbar as well.

But just recently, you have the opportunity to use this when you enter the File Explorer window.

To do this:

1. Enter the **Settings**

2. Choose **Personalization**

3. Select **Colors**

4. When you scroll to the bottom, you will see the option to **Choose Your Default App Mode**. Change this to dark.

#TRICK 17
Light mode

For many apps and devices, you find the option for Dark mode. But with a very recent update that the Windows 10 got, the Light mode has been returned.

With this new **Light mode** in Windows 10, the display will be a little easier on the eyes.

You find this in the Display settings and you can set it to work for particular apps and components.

When you use the custom option you are able to set Dark or Light mode for specific elements in the Operating System.

#TRICK 18

The new Clipboard

The feature of Clipboard has been created for a long time now and has received little updates. At least not until now.

With an update in 2018, Microsoft decided to bring some really cool options.

If you have that update, you can reach this;

    1. Enter the **Settings**

    2. Go to **System**

3. Select **Clipboard**.

4. If you want to save different items to this Clipboard, you can just enable **Clipboard History**.

#TRICK 19
Capture with the screen capture tool

There have been many updates for the Windows 10 and this OS just keeps getting better. Some say that the feature of **Screen Capture** has made the Windows 10 a worthy competitor of the macOS. The Windows 10 got this is the update in October 2018.

This is not the Snipping Tool that you already know of. This is the new feature **Snip & Sketch**.

If you would like to access this, you just have to hit **Shift + Windows key + S**. This will enable you to take a rectangular or full screen capture.

It's great feature that you can quickly use when you need to capture something.

#TRICK 20

The unknown game bar

When you hit **Windows key + G**, you are able to fire up the new game bar. With this, you can enter game mode with your PC.

What this means is that notifications are turned off, resources are pulled into the game and you can broadcast the game.

If you would like to configure some keyboard shortcuts, you can just hit the Start menu and search for the Game Bar. You can set shortcuts to turn off recording timer, screen capture or microphone as you are gaming.

SECTION FOUR

WINDOWS 10 SHORTCUTS

CHAPTER 9

40 Windows 10 Shortcuts

Using shortcuts on the Windows 10 is a very fast way for you to increase your productivity when you work.

Here, we'll discuss the **top Windows 10 shortcuts** that will get you to switch between Windows, split the screens, do some multitasking in desktop and others.

Learning the keyboard shortcuts is like learning a new language. And just like learning a language, you don't always master it all at first. So do not worry.

You'll start small as you build up your vocabulary. In time you'll get to understand and speak the language well.

So it is with the shortcuts for your Windows 10, you want to begin building your vocabulary with the things that you do regularly like switching from one program to another. When you do it often it'll stick to your memory and you'll remember.

Some of the things that you can learn first is minimizing Windows, looking for programs, multitasking through files, getting along with Windows search and finding some documents and files.

When you start to learn your shortcuts with the actions that you make use of regularly, you'll build your confidence with shortcut, speed up the activities that you carry out in Windows 10 and you'll get motivated to learn more since you're already seeing success with the small tasks.

SHORTCUT 1

❖ Windows key + 1 or another number

Take a look at the taskbar, what you'll see is a row of applications and programs lined up. If you have an app that you make use of more frequently than others, you can just add it to the row. In fact, you could add it to the first place.

So let's say that **Google Chrome** is as the first app on your taskbar, you can just press **Windows key + 1** to get it open.

You can also try this with other apps. Like if an app is in the 3rd position, you can just use **Windows key + 3** to open it up. The point is made clear: the number you pick represents the position of the app you wish to open in the row.

If you would like to add your favorite app to the taskbar, follow these steps:

1. Press the **Win** key and enter in the name of the app

2. Right-click the app

3. Choose the option for **Pin to taskbar**

4. The app will now be in the taskbar. You can also click and drag it to any position you want to on the taskbar

So you can add any program (except the File Explorer) to the taskbar and move it to any position you want.

The reason you don't want to add the File Explorer is because it already has its own shortcut.

We'll talk a bit more on this in a short while

SHORTCUT 2

❖ Windows key + left

There are variations to this command, you can also try **Windows key + right, Windows key + up** and **Windows key + down.**

What they all do is that they send the window or program that is currently open to the side of the screen. The left and right commands will send it to the left and right of the screen while the up and down commands will send the window reduce the size to the top and bottom of the screen.

If you have 2 apps opened and you click **Windows key + left** or **Windows key + right** for a particular app, you'll be asked to set the other app to fill the empty area of the screen.

SHORTCUT 3

❖ <u>Windows key then type or Ctrl + E then type</u>

The search option that exists in Windows is like the best thing ever. It definitely gets top rank in the list of useful searches. The reason for this is that you can basically find anything through it.

With this option, you don't have to fiddle around trying to find a particular file or app. You just use the search.

All you do is press the **Win key** and input the name of the program of app that you're looking for and it'll show up. It has no excuse not to.

In fact, you don't have to include the full name of the program before Windows brings it out to you.

I looked for **Google Chrome** and all I did was type in '**Go**' and it supplies it at the top of the list.

SHORTCUT 4

❖ <u>Alt + F</u>

This is a cool way to enter the file menu options in a program. Like for example in Microsoft word, where you have the **File, Home, Insert** and others. The **Alt + F** option will enable you to open the file menu.

It is kind of a stress to scroll all the way to the top just to reach the file option.

And it's not only the file you can reach with a shortcut.

When you press the **Alt** key, you'll see the key that you need to press to get the other options to show.

Still in Microsoft word and you press the **Alt** key. It will alert you that **Alt + H** will enter the **Home** and **Alt + N** will open **Insert**.

SHORTCUT 5

❖ Ctrl + Shift + Esc

This will get you to open the task manager quickly.

You can also try to enter the search and type in '**Task Manager**'.

But the **Ctrl + Shift + Esc** option is quicker.

SHORTCUT 6

❖ **Alt + Enter**

When you select a file or a document and you want to see the properties, you don't have to right click and choose **Properties**.

You can just easily press **Alt + Enter** and the properties window will open up.

It's in this "properties: segment that you'll be able to see the size of the file, the date when it was created, date it was modified and other properties of the file.

Another shortcut to summon the **properties window** is to use **Alt + right click**. It does the same thing; bring up the properties menu.

SHORTCUT 7

❖ <u>Windows key + E</u>

When it comes to looking for apps and programs, the best place to turn to is the Windows search.

But when it comes to looking for files and documents, the File Explorer is great at it.

The reason for this is not only because the name says **'File' Explorer** but also because it does some filtering features that allow users to be able to narrow down what they search for. This method is an efficient way to dig through and find files in your computer.

For you to summon the File Explorer in shortcut style, you just use **Windows key + E**. Now you'll see a wide array of options that you use to search for your file. You'll see navigational options, filers and views that you can use to improve your 'search experience'

In the search bar at the top right, you can input the name of a file you want to find.

But something else that you can try to do again is to input the extension of a file. Like you add **the .jpg or .png** if you are looking for a photo. Or, you can find a document with the **.docx** extension

SHORTCUT 8

❖ Windows key + Ctrl + D

This button will help you to create another desktop.

And by another desktop, it's a virtual one.

SHORTCUT 9

❖ <u>Windows key + Ctrl + left or right</u>

This will help to go navigate through the desktops. Pressing the left key will return to the previous desktops you were in.

Pressing the right key will navigatel you through the newer desktops you just created.

SHORTCUT 10

❖ Windows key + Ctrl + F4

What of when you're done with the virtual desktop, you want to close it, but you have no idea how?

You just have to press **Windows key + Ctrl + F4** to quit it.

Just make sure that you have saved all what you were doing on the new desktop.

SHORTCUT 11

❖ <u>Ctrl + E</u>

Lovely way to turn on the search. You can make use of this option in the File Explorer. This will help you to search the current folder you are in.

When you hit the **Ctrl + E** option on your keyboard, the cursor will jump to the search box at the right hand corner of the screen. So you have a fast way to search for a file. Just press **Windows key + E** to enter

File Explorer and **Ctrl + E** to search for the item.

This doesn't only work in File Explorer. It will also work when you are in a web browser (or at least for most modern browser).

Try it for Microsoft Edge or Google Chrome. Pressing the **Ctrl + E** will send you to the address bar for you to enter the any URL.

SHORTCUT 12

❖ Windows key + X

This option will get you to open up the start menu options. Normally you would have to right click the **Start** to show up this menu.

This is the menu that houses the mobility center, program and features, device manager, task manager and more.

SHORTCUT 13

❖ Windows key + I

This is a quick way to launch the **Settings** window.

If you are looking for a particular setting, you can use the search to find it.

SHORTCUT 14

❖ **Alt + Tab**

Another shortcut that makes this list among is the **Alt + Tab** function. What this does is that it enables you switch between Windows very quickly.

Let's say that you are working on Microsoft Word and Google Chrome. Normally, you'll have to go to the bottom of the taskbar to select the program you want to switch to or you can just minimize the current program you're in to get to the other one.

But with the **Alt + Tab** option you can switch easily. You can press the combo once and then you'll go to the other program that's opened.

You can also press it again to switch back to the previous window. That's for 2 programs. What happens when there are 3 or more programs opened?

Easy enough! When there are multiple programs opened, pressing the **Alt + E** option won't get you to switch between all of them. All you have to do is to hold down the **Alt** button and then press the **Tab** continuously till it navigates to your desired window.

As you press the **Tab**. Don't release the **Alt** key.

SHORTCUT 15

❖ Ctrl + Alt + Tab

This one is just like the option we just talked about. Except, you won't have to hold down the **Alt + key.**

When you press this combo, all the windows will be opened to you just like the **Alt** key will do but this time, it will remain like that.

This is also known as the **Tab Switch Freeze**. Instead of letting you to just jump between windows and programs you just opened recently, you'll be able to see all the items that you've opened on your computer.

Then you can then switch to the one you would like to open. You can make use of the same **Tab** key or you could use the left and right controls to navigate through the windows

SHORTCUT 16

❖ Windows key + R

This will have you opening up the **Run** dialog box

SHORTCUT 17

❖ Windows key + A

When you get notifications they show up at the edge of your screen for a few seconds. You have those few seconds to select it and attend to the matter. If you wait any longer, it will disappear.

But you can still access the notification by going to the **Action Center**.

Normally you have to go the corner of the display to access it. It is the icon that's just before the Date and Time. Yes, that one.

But the problem with that is it's too far. With **Windows key + A**, you'll get to it much faster. Just press it once and the Action Center opens up.

SHORTCUT 18

❖ Windows key + T

This is another method of switching through Windows. When you press the **Windows key + T**. you'll move through the options in the taskbar.

As you press **T** continuously, you'll see the taskbar run through the items on it. When it eventually gets to the app you want just hit **Enter** to open it up.

SHORTCUT 19

❖ <u>Alt + left or right</u>

If you've opened many folders in File Explorer and you want to go back, this is a great option. Just hold the **Alt + left** and press left to go back.

You can press the **Alt + right** to return to the folder you've just closed.

You should know that this shortcut will only get you to move through the folders that you've opened before. That is your search history. They will not get you to folders unless you have actually opened the folder before.

If you want to move a folder hierarchy. (That is the folder that houses the current folder you are in) you can just use **Alt + up**.

This shortcut does not just work for File Explorer only. The **Alt + right** and **Alt + left** shortcut can also work when you in a web browser. You'll be able to move forwards and backwards through the history of what you've searched for in the same tab.

No more looking for the back button on the screen, **Alt + left** does the trick. This works for most browsers like Chrome, Edge and Firefox.

SHORTCUT 20

❖ Windows key + ,

It just gets better. If you would like to see the desktop and not minimize your apps this is the way to go

Pressing **Windows key + ,** will get you to see the desktop briefly and return to your program. The longer you hold Windows key the longer the desktop stays.

SHORTCUT 21

❖ Right-click taskbar + D

This is a good option to see what's going on in the computer if you opened different programs.

All you have to do is just **Right-click the taskbar at the bottom of screen and then press D**

When you do this all the opened windows will be in cascade. That is, they'll be stocked behind each other. When you use this cascade formation, you'll be able to find the apps that are open. If there's a program you don't want to use again, you can close it.

SHORTCUT 22

❖ Right-click taskbar + U.

So you just tried the shortcut to cascade the windows. It worked, the windows are stacked behind each other now you want to get out of the mode.

You easily opt-out of the cascade option for the windows **by Right-clicking on the taskbar then pressing U.** this will revert the windows to the normal view and undo the cascade effect.

Before you can actually do the **'uncascade'** windows option, you should have used the cascade option first.

SHORTCUT 23

❖ Right-click taskbar + E

The cascading option is great to see which programs are open on your computer.

But there's a better way. It is the option to show windows stacked side-by-side. This does what it says. Its stacks the windows that are open.

All you have to do is **Right-click the taskbar then press E.** The way in which the windows will be stacked on your computer will depend on the number of apps or programs that you have opened and the type of documents and files that you have opened.

The windows will not be snapped to the corners, they'll just be resized and stacked.

If you stacked the windows, and it has already served its purpose, you can always revert it back to the window you were in by **Right-clicking the taskbar then pressing U**.

SHORTCUT 24

❖ Ctrl + F6

So let's say that you have two documents opened in Microsoft word. The normal way that you switch between them is by moving to the taskbar at the bottom, click the app icon then choose the document to enter.

Nice way. But too slow and it does reduce productivity.

A quicker way; **Ctrl + F6**. This is the cycle program shortcut that will switch to the files that you opened for the same program.

If you opened, say 9 documents in Microsoft word, you can just press the **Ctrl + F6** and it will switch to the next document.

Don't release the Ctrl and keep **pressing F6**. You'll see that it just keeps cycling through the files you opened.

SHORTCUT 25

❖ Windows key + PrtSc

If you want to take screenshot on your computer, you can just press the **PrtSc** button on the keyboard. But that won't save it to the computer

Press **Windows key + PrtSc** and you'll be able to view the screenshot page in the pictures folder

SHORTCUT 26

❖ **Ctrl + M**

Another option that you want to make use of to minimize all windows is the **Ctrl + M** shortcut. When you have many windows opened, minimizing them one after the other with the minimize button at the top can be stressful

Especially when you have about 10 windows opened at once. **Ctrl + M** minimizes them all at once.

SHORTCUT 27

❖ Ctrl + W

As you work with many files that are opened in Windows 10, you may want to close a document but not out of the program itself. That was what this shortcut was made.

When you hit **Ctrl + W**, the current files that you make use of will be closed but the app will still be open.

What this means is if you hit **Ctrl + W** on a word document, the current files will be closed but Microsoft word itself will still be opened. You can then open another file. You will also be given two options; Save or Don't Save

You also make use of this **Ctrl + W** shortcut when you're in multitasking view. You'll be able to use it to close any files that is opened at that moment.

SHORTCUT 28

❖ Alt + F4

This shortcut should not be mistaken for **Ctrl + W**. The **Alt + F4** shortcut will not only quit the current file that you are working on but it will close you out of the application itself. When you press it, you'll also be given the option for **Save or Don't Save**.

When you press the **Alt + F4** on a word document, Windows will close any word document that is opened and also close Microsoft word. This very different from the **Ctrl + W** that only closes you out of the current file that is opened.

But that's not the only thing **Alt + F4** does. If you are on your windows desktop and you press the **Alt + F4** shortcut, you'll get the option to shut down your computer.

If you are working on a file and you want to shutdown very quickly, you can just press **Ctrl + M** to minimize all the windows that are opened, then press **Alt + F4** to shut down your computer

SHORTCUT 29

❖ Alt + Shift + D

This is a great way to insert the date very quickly. Pressing **Alt + Shift + D** will paste the date in format set is in your computer.

Alt + Shift + T will get to paste the current time where the cursor is in a document.

SHORTCUT 30

❖ Ctrl + N

When you're in Microsoft office suite, go-to option for creating a new document should be the **Ctrl + N** shortcut. You can create new blank files very quickly and easily.

So if you are working on Microsoft PowerPoint and you hit the **Ctrl + N**, a new presentation that you can work with will be opened for you.

Ctrl + N is also be very useful when you're managing your files with the Windows File Explorer.

When you press the combo from File Explorer, you'll be given a new window that you can work with.

Now you have 2 windows for the File Explorer. Snap it to split screen and you'll be able to drag and drop files into different folders.

If you created a window by opening Windows File Explorer afresh, you'll be shown the homepage. But by using Ctrl + N, you'll be given a replica of the folder you're in but in a different window.

SHORTCUT 31

❖ Ctrl + Shift + N

Still on File Explorer hacks. If you are in a folder and you want to create a new folder, you just have to hit **Ctrl + Shift + N** and a new blank folder will be created.

With this method you can easily create folders on the fly without stress. You'll be able to organize files quicker leading to better productivity.

Normally you will have to **right click an empty space in the file explorer, chose New, then select folder**. That method is long and stressful. It even makes one reconsider creating a new folder when one thinks of the process he has to go through.

But now, **Ctrl + Shift + N** makes it ever easier

SHORTCUT 32

❖ **Ctrl + Shift + >**

This is a quick way to increase the size of a text. Instead of moving all the way up simply pressing **Ctrl + Shift + >** will do the trick

SHORTCUT 33

❖ Ctrl + Shift + <

With **Ctrl + Shift + >**, you'll be able to decrease the size of the selected text.

To decrease the size even further, keep pressing the **>** while the Ctrl + Shift is still held down

SHORTCUT 34

❖ Right click + W + document

Creating a new folder with **Ctrl + Shift + N** is a fast and easy way to create empty folders. But what if you want to create new file without entering the program.

Yes it is possible to create a new document and not get into the application itself. You can do this for any Microsoft office application.

If you want to create a new blank document of an application, you just have to:

1. Right click an area in the folder you want to the document to be

2. Press **W** to get to the New option

3. Choose the type of file you want to open

When you choose the file type, you'll see that a new document of the application will be created. It will have the default name so you may have to enter a new one.

The file is created. And you did all this without having to open the application itself.

SHORTCUT 35

❖ Windows key + +

Have you been finding yourself squinting to find out what is written on the screen of your computer?

You may enlarged the text size for the application but maybe that's not enough or you don't want it zoomed in permanently.

Your next option is to use the **Windows key + +** shortcut. When you press the combo, you'll see that the items on your screen will become magnified. That's because you just opened the magnifier.

If you want to get a more zoomed in view you keep pressing **the +**. Just make sure that you don't release the Windows key.

SHORTCUT 36

❖ Windows key + -

This does the same as the previous shortcut; magnifier. Except this one does the opposite; it zooms out. The zooming out does not happen when you're in the normal view of the screen.

There nothing to zoom out from at that point. But when you use the **Windows key + +** shortcut, you can easily use the **Windows key + +** shortcut to reverse the effect.

SHORTCUT 37

❖ Ctrl + End

If you are using Microsoft word or any other word editing program, one easy way to go the end of the is to use **Ctrl + End**.

The normal way to do it is by using the slider at the right side of the page. Then you drag it to the end, but that's okay.

But why would you use that when you've got **Ctrl + End**?!

SHORTCUT 38

❖ Ctrl + Home

This is the opposite of the last shortcut.

You'll be able to use the **Ctrl + Home** shortcut to move directly to the beginning of the document.

SHORTCUT 39

❖ Shift + Home

When you want to highlight a document in word, the normal procedure is to click and drag to the end of the word.

Not only is that method slow when it comes to highlighting all the texts in the same line, but you can select something else.

The **Shift + Home** shortcut makes it easier.

When you use the shortcut, the word from the cursor to the beginning of the line will be selected.

SHORTCUT 40

❖ Shift + End.

This does the opposite of the previous shortcut. **Shift + End** will highlight from the end of the text to where the cursor is.

DISCLAIMER

This book only contains tricks and shortcuts that works exclusively for the Windows OS; most especially the Windows 10.

The author is not to be held responsible if the shortcuts and tricks are used on other OS and they caused a system malfunction.

About the Author

Peter Maxwell has been a certified apps developer and tech researcher for more than 17 years.

Some of his "How to" guides have appeared in a handful of international journals and tech blogs.

Printed in Great Britain
by Amazon